Our
Broken World

kevin mayhew

To Glyn and Susan Jones and family,
with love and gratitude for good times shared

First published in 2005 by

KEVIN MAYHEW LTD
Buxhall, Stowmarket, Suffolk, IP14 3BW
E-mail: info@kevinmayhewltd.com

9 8 7 6 5 4 3 2 1 0

ISBN 1 84417 366 6
Catalogue No. 1500770

Designed by Chris Coe

Printed and bound in China

Contents

Introduction

Is the world of the twenty-first century any more broken than that of years gone by? We live today under the shadow of terrorism, with an attendant increase in racial and religious tension, but past centuries have had their own evils: Christians fed to the lions in ancient Rome; the Black Death sweeping across Europe in the Middle Ages; burnings of Catholics and Protestants under the Tudors; carnage on the battlefields of the First World War; and mass murder of Jews during the Holocaust. Brokenness, in other words, is nothing new. These, of course, are just the tip of the iceberg – some of the darkest moments in a world that is daily scarred by evil, sorrow and suffering. Just like us today, past generations have struggled to make sense of their faith in the context of events unfolding before them – the harsh realities of life – striving to understand how one can talk of a loving God amid so much that seems to question or deny his presence.

There are no easy answers to such conundrums, and this book doesn't purport to offer any. All we can do sometimes is pray, offering our questions, concerns, troubles and doubts to God in the conviction that he hears and responds. It isn't always apparent how, when or where, but that serves to bring us back to the fact that we live in an imperfect world, one in which God's purpose is repeatedly frustrated, his love obscured and his hands tied. Though we struggle to explain it, we believe that he grieves at our plight as much as any, and that, despite all that conspires against him, the time will come when wrong will be righted, good will conquer evil and his kingdom will come. The prayers in this collection attempt to articulate some of those ideas, giving voice both to our confusion and to our faith.

But why poetry? The answer is very simple. For me, verse — and rhyming verse in particular — is able to express things in a way that prose alone cannot quite match. The rhythm carries the reader along, the rhyme gives a sense of completeness and final resolution, and the two in tandem make the words easy to remember and repeat. These prayers, then, or poems — call them what you will — aim to express some of the feelings you may have in the light of our world today, in all its need and pain. They are offered, quite simply, to help you pray.

Nick Fawcett

A Divided World

**How good and precious it is when
people live together in unity.**
Psalm 133:1

Lord, to our world in its madness –
broken, bemused and concussed,
crushed by a burden of sadness,
ravaged by fear and mistrust –
grant your renewal and healing,
courage where hope seems in vain,
reach out to all who are reeling,
bring them relief from their pain;
break down the roots of division,
walls that destroy and estrange;
overcome hate and suspicion,
grant us the prospect of change.

Behind the Labels

**There can be neither Jew nor Greek, slave
nor free, male nor female, for you are all one
in Jesus Christ.**
Galatians 3:28

Lord, for using labels to decide on people's worth:
their age, their sex, their class, their roots,
their faith or place of birth,
their politics or culture, the colour of their skin,
the outward signs that mark them out
instead of what's within;
for summing people up by what nobody can change –
allowing background, creed or race
to poison and estrange –
for all such prejudice, forgive, and from it set me free
to meet the person underneath –
to look and really see.

A World in Need

**He empathises with the vulnerable
and those in need, reaching out to save.**
Psalm 72:12

In a world of hurt and need,
scarred by selfishness and greed;
touched by sorrow, racked by pain,
such that hope can seem in vain;
in this mix of toil and strife
where so much devalues life;
gracious Lord, I pray be there,
show to all how much you care.

Faith in Action

**Not everyone saying to me, 'Lord, Lord'
will enter the kingdom of heaven, but only
those who do the will of my heavenly Father.**
Matthew 7:21

Save me from empty pleas, Lord,
from prayers that are short on deeds,
from claiming to care for others
but ignoring their basic needs.
Save me from false religion
which seeks only that souls are fed –
too quick to offer the gospel,
too slow to give daily bread.
Fill me with Christ's compassion,
inspire me freely to give,
to share with joy from my plenty
that others might simply live.

Praying for Others

**Whenever you responded to the least
of your brothers and sisters,
you responded also to me.**
Matthew 25:40

Hear my prayer for others
in the trials they face –
fellow sisters, brothers:
grant to all your grace.
Heal the crushed and broken,
body, mind and soul –
let your word be spoken
touch and make them whole.

Chide the rich and greedy,
strengthen the oppressed,
reach out to the needy,
comfort the distressed.
May the humble flourish
may the poor be fed,
in your mercy nourish
all who crave for bread.
Bring to every nation
harmony once more,
reconciliation,
peace instead of war.
Hear my intercession,
make my life a prayer;
help me give expression
to your love and care.

Faith and Doubt

Why, Lord, are you so distant?
Why do you conceal yourself
in times of difficulty?
Psalm 10:1

What is the truth I'm seeking?
What do I hope to find?
Is it your voice that's speaking
or just some trick of the mind?
Why don't you hear my crying?
Why don't you answer prayer?
Why is the child dying?
Why don't you seem to care?
So much in life bemuses,
turning my faith to doubt;
so much obscures and confuses –
Lord, I can't work it out.

How can we call you caring
faced by such sorrow and pain?
Is there not cause for despairing
when all our hopes seem in vain?
Lord, have you any suggestions?
Can all these riddles make sense?
I cannot stifle my questions,
cannot indulge in pretence.
Where rival answers are warring,
where I just don't understand,
teach me to keep on exploring,
striving to make out your hand.
Help me to search sincerely,
baring my soul to you;
even though *I* can't see clearly,
help me to trust that *you* do.

The Riddle of Life

**Why do you let me witness wrongdoing
and endure trouble? Destruction
and aggression are all around me;
conflicts and disputes spring up everywhere.
The law is watered down such that justice
has no chance of winning through.**
Habakkuk 1:3-4a

Lord, I see such goodness,
yet such evil too:
much that makes me question,
much that speaks of you.
All around are riddles
hard to understand –
help me find some answers,
help me see your hand.

Where there's pain and sorrow,
where your children bleed,
where there seems no future
for a world in need,
break into the darkness,
bring an end to night,
show that love continues,
shine again your light.
Though my faith is shaken,
hope appearing vain,
though belief is battered,
sorely under strain,
give me strength to trust you,
courage to hold out;
show me that you're present;
speak, Lord, in my doubt.

One People?

I pray for all those who will believe in me ...
that they may all be one, as we are one,
I living in them as you live in me, in order
that they may become so completely united
that the world is left in no doubt that you sent me
and love them, just as you have loved me.
John 17:20b, 21b, 23

You've called us as your Church, Lord, your people here on earth,
a fellowship of equals where all are given worth,
a family together, distinguished by our care,
one faith, one hope, one gospel, one vision that we share.
Yet we have been divided by doctrine, dogma, creed,
estranged from one another – we've left your wounds to bleed.

Too full of our convictions, believing others wrong,
we've lost sight of the body to which we all belong.
Our differences deny you, betray the faith we claim;
instead of love uniting, we squabble in your name.
Lord, heal the wounds that scar us – suspicion, fear and pride;
reveal the good in others that all our labels hide.
May cords of love unite us, too strong to be undone –
although we may be many, equip us to be one.

Questions of Faith

Lord, I believe; conquer my unbelief.
Mark 9:24

Lord, there are times when I need to ask, 'Why?' –
times when appearances give faith the lie.
Innocents suffer and evil holds sway.
Grant me some answers, Lord, teach me your way.

Lord, there are times when I need to ask, 'Where?' –
times when it seems that you simply don't care.
Though I call out, you seem distant, aloof.
Show me you're present, Lord, grant me some proof.

Lord, there are times when I need to ask, 'What?' –
    times when your hand isn't easy to spot.
What is life's purpose and what of me here?
In my confusion, Lord, make your will clear.

Lord, there are times when I need to ask, 'How?' –
    times when your promises clash with life now.
Wrestling with doubt I ask, 'How can this be?'
Give me some insight, Lord, help me to see.

Lord, there are times when the questions run fast –
    times when I fear that my faith might not last.
Hear me, support me, and help me get through.
Lead me through darkness till light shines anew.

For Those Who Care
Enough to Show It

**Learn to do good, seek justice,
encourage the oppressed, defend the cause of
the fatherless, plead the case of the widow.**
Isaiah 1:17

For those who fight injustice
and make a stand for good,
who strive to give the poor a chance
to live life as they should,
for all who labour, heart and soul,
to make our world more fair,
I ask your courage, succour, strength –
Lord, answer, hear my prayer.

For those who show compassion,
who work to heal and mend,
who nurse the sick, support the weak,
encourage and befriend,
for all who reach out in your name
to offer love and care,
I ask your blessing, power, help –
Lord, answer, hear my prayer.

For those who tackle conflict,
where wounds run red and raw,
who strive to conquer hatred
and put a stop to war,
who work to foster dialogue
despite the scars we bear,
I ask your guidance, vision, faith –
Lord, answer, hear my prayer.

For those who try to witness
to Christ through word and deed,
to show his love embraces
each colour, culture, creed,
who point to light and life and hope
in which we all can share,
I ask your wisdom, grace and truth –
Lord, answer, hear my prayer.

When God Seems Distant

Tears are my food day and night,
while people keep on saying to me,
'Where is your God?'
Psalm 42:3

Where were you, Lord, when the planes struck
and the towers came crashing down?
What did you do to stop it?
Why were you out of town?
Where were you in the Balkans
when the streets ran red with blood?
And how about the shanty town
engulfed by streams of mud?
Why don't you end the famine?
Why don't you stop the war?
How can you let these happen?
What can it all be for?

Lord, is it wrong to ask you,
faithless to speak my mind?
Shouldn't I look for answers?
Don't you say 'seek and find'?
Yes, I know much is beyond me,
truth often hard to discern,
but I'm ready and willing to listen,
eager and hungry to learn.
Don't think I'm daring to judge you,
set myself up in your place –
some things, I know, must stay hidden,
at least till we meet face to face –
yet in a world where so many
feel faith and hope are in vain,
give us some sign, Lord, I beg you
to prove you are here in our pain.

Hope in Times of Confusion

**I am convinced that nothing will ever be able
to separate us from Christ's love.
Neither death nor life, neither angels nor
demons, neither the present nor the future,
neither any powers, height or depth,
nor indeed anything else in all creation,
will ever be able to separate us from the love
of God that is ours in Christ Jesus our Lord.**
Romans 8:38-39

Though much in life bemuses
or flatters to deceive;
though what we face confuses,
denies what we believe;
though confidence is shattered
when evil wins the day,
and all our hopes seem battered,
our troubles here to stay;

though fortune leaves us shaken,
destroying every dream;
new faith, Lord, reawaken
that things aren't what they seem.
Assure us you are turning
the darkness into light,
that grace will keep on burning,
however deep the night.
Revive, restore, refresh us
when trust and vision pall –
renew the faith – so precious –
that love will conquer all.

For the Elderly and Infirm

**Our life expectancy is seventy years,
eighty if we're lucky, and of that fleeting span
a large part brings trial and tribulation.
Our years fly past, and life races by in tandem.**

Psalm 90:10

Reach out to those who are ageing,
all for whom life is a strain,
those who are constantly waging
war against illness and pain.
Comfort the troubled and tearful,
give them your help to get by.
Strengthen those worried and fearful,
lovingly answer their cry.

Nurture the broken and ailing –
bodies grown weary and old,
faculties steadily failing –
scared what the future might hold.
Help those who, friendless and lonely,
wish that each day were their last,
those who find happiness only
when thinking of moments long past.
Lord, though the years lead to testing,
often too bitter to bear,
leaving some sadly protesting,
feeling you no longer care,
show that the future's not finished,
that your love still offers more,
carrying on undiminished,
holding the best things in store.

The Shadow of Death

**Blessed are those who mourn;
they will be comforted.**
Matthew 5:4

Lord, I pray for those who grieve,
mourning those they've loved and lost;
tears their lot, without reprieve,
joy extracting such a cost;
each day bringing added pain,
memories of times they knew,
never to be shared again –
life a case of getting through.

When their hearts are fit to break –
hurt too bitter to express –
grant them solace, dull the ache,
comfort them in their distress.
In their anger, loss and shock,
help them find in you a friend;
in their turmoil be their rock,
one on whom they can depend.
Though they feel they cannot cope,
gracious God, reach out to save;
bring to each new life, new hope
in your love, beyond the grave.

Our Eternal Home

Then I saw a new heaven and earth;
for the first heaven and earth,
together with the sea, had come to an end.
There will be no more night, nor need of any
light from a lamp or the sun, for the
Lord God will be their light, and they will
reign forevermore.
Revelation 21:1; 22:5

Grant, Lord, an end to our sorrow,
a halt at last to our pain,
the hope of a brighter tomorrow,
of sunshine, after the rain.

Assure us the day is dawning
when darkness will be no more,
no suffering, dying or mourning,
no violence, hatred or war –
a kingdom of joy unbounded,
of laughter, blessing and peace,
where evil will be confounded
and all divisions cease;
a time of celebration,
a place of rare delights –
Lord, finish your new creation
and set our world to rights.